#dream

a quote book

by gloria marie pelcher

Copyright © 2014 Gloria Marie Pelcher

All rights reserved. No portion of this book may be used or reproduced in any manner whatsoever without written permission of the author or Creative Bluebird except in the case of brief quotations embodied in critical articles and reviews.

#dream: a quote book

ISBN-13: 978-0692330876 (Creative Bluebird)

ISBN-10: 0692330879

#quotebooks is a trademark of

Creative Bluebird
www.creativebluebird.com

For book inquiries please visit
creativebluebird.com/contact

for

___

from

___

date

___

#dream

Here's to living your dreams! Fuel to help you chase down your dreams, to increase your tenacity to go after them with everything you have.

There is only one thing that makes a dream impossible to achieve: the fear of failure.
Paulo Coelho

Dare to live the life you have dreamed for yourself. Go forward and make your dreams come true.

Ralph Waldo Emerson

Those who give up dreams, do injury to their own hearts and cannot possibly enjoy a profound sense of fulfillment in the end.

Daisaku Ikeda

We are the music-makers,
and we are the Dreamers of
Dreams.
Willy Wonka

Dreams are stories made by and for the dreamer, and each dreamer has his own folds to open and knots to untie.

Siri Hustvedt

Obstacles are those frightful things you see when you take your eyes off your goal.

Henry Ford

If one dream should fall and break into a thousand pieces, never be afraid to pick one of those pieces up and begin again.

Flavia Weedn

Dream your dream; and realize that you are more than just the dreamer, you are the point of origin for its reality.

Steve Maraboli

Never quit on your one and only dream!!!

Raven Kaldera

I've dreamt in my life dreams that have stayed with me ever after, and changed my ideas: they've gone through and through me, like wine through water, and altered the colour of my mind.

Emily Brontë

I wasn't going to be one of those people who died wondering what if? I would keep putting my dreams to the test - even though it meant living with uncertainty and fear of failure. This is the shadowland of hope, and anyone with a dream must learn to live there.

Alex Haley

Dream as if you'll live forever. Live as if you'll die tomorrow.

James Dean

Whatever you do, or dream you can, begin it. Boldness has genius and power and magic in it.

Johann Wolfgang von Goethe

Fully inhale your dream and completely exhale manifestation of it.
>
> T.F. Hodge

A head full of fears has no space for dreams.

Author Unknown

I grew up with an ambition and determination without which I would have been a good deal happier. I thought a lot and developed the faraway look of a dreamer, for it was always the distant heights that fascinated me and drew me to them in spirit. I was not sure what could be accomplished with tenacity and little else, but the target was set high and each rebuff only saw me more determined to see at least one major dream to its fulfillment.

Earl Denman

A #2 pencil and a dream can take you anywhere.

                                             Joyce A. Myers

Only you can hold yourself back, only you can stand in your own way, only you can help yourself.

Mikhail Strabo

Just go out there and do what you've got to do.

Martina Navratilo

Never give up on a dream just because of the time it will take to accomplish it. The time will pass anyway.
Earl Nightingale

Doing new and different things doesn't always work, but if you don't try, you'll never do anything in a big way.

Jean Feiwel

Walk with the dreamers, the believers, the courageous, the cheerful, the planners, the doers, the successful people with their heads in the clouds and their feet on the ground. Let their spirit ignite a fire within you to leave this world better than when you found it…

Wilferd Peterson

The future belongs to those who believe in the beauty of their dreams.

Eleanor Roosevelt

Hold fast to dreams,
For if dreams die
Life is a broken-winged bird,
That cannot fly.

Langston Hughes

Throw your dreams into space like a kite, and you do not know what it will bring back, a new life, a new friend, a new love, a new country.
Anaïs Nin

Let go of the past and go for the future. Go confidently in the direction of your dreams. Live the life you imagined.
 Henry David Thoreau

Twenty years from now you will be more disappointed by the things that you didn't do than by the ones you did do. So throw off the bowlines, sail away from safe harbor, catch the trade winds in your sails, explore, dream, discover.

Mark Twain

No person has the right to
rain on your dreams.
Martin Luther King Jr.

To dream is to starve doubt, feed hope.

Justina Chen

Dreams, if they're any good,
are always a little bit crazy.
                                Ray Charles

The inability to open up to hope is what blocks trust, and blocked trust is the reason for blighted dreams.

Elizabeth Gilbert

When we can't dream any longer we die.

                                                  Emma Goldman

I want to be around people that do things. I don't want to be around people anymore that judge or talk about what people do. I want to be around people that dream and support and do things.

Amy Poehler

It takes a lot of courage to show your dreams to someone else.

        Erma Bombeck

Thank God even crazy dreams come true

Carrie Underwood

If you have a dream, don't just sit there. Gather courage to believe that you can succeed and leave no stone unturned to make it a reality.
Roopleen

Sometimes Life Is About Risking Everything For A Dream No One Can See But You

                                                      Unknown

Dreams are extremely important. You can't do it unless you imagine it.

George Lucas

Goals are dreams with deadlines.

Diana Scharf

Follow your Dreams - They give pathway to the wonder of who you are.

Debbie Burns

Stop sharing your dreams with people who try to hold you back, even if they're your parents.

Kelly Cutrone

Don't be afraid of the space between your dreams and reality. If you can dream it, you can make it so.

Belva Davis

You must give everything to make your life as beautiful as the dreams that dance in your imagination.

Roman Payne

We may place blame, give reasons, and even have excuses; but in the end, it is an act of cowardice to not follow your dreams.

Steve Maraboli

Maybe we could all take care of each other, I dreamed.
Michelle Tea

I'd rather fail miserably pursuing my dreams than succeed at something I have to settle for

Katie Kacvinsky

Not much happens without a dream. And for something great to happen, there must be a great dream. Behind every great achievement is a dreamer of great dreams. Much more than a dreamer is required to bring it to reality; but the dream must be there first.

Robert K. Greenleaf

We need men who can dream of things that never were.
John F. Kennedy

There is hope in dreams, imagination, and in the courage of those who wish to make those dreams a reality.
Jonas Salk

Every morning you have two choices. Continue to sleep with your dreams or wake up and chase them.

Unknown

my favorite dream quote

_____
_____
_____
_____
_____
_____
_____
_____
_____
_____

ABOUT *this book*

THIS BOOK that you are holding in your hands was made with love by GLORIA MARIE PELCHER. This book is part of the *#quotebooks*™ collection of books. This book is perfectly okay with being loved, bought, read, reread, shared, gifted, tweeted, instagrammed, liked, reviewed, borrowed, and of course quoted.

gloriamarie.com/quotebooks

FB / IG / Twitter: @gloriamarie

www.ingramcontent.com/pod-product-compliance
Lightning Source LLC
Chambersburg PA
CBHW070459050426
42449CB00012B/3045